D0938129

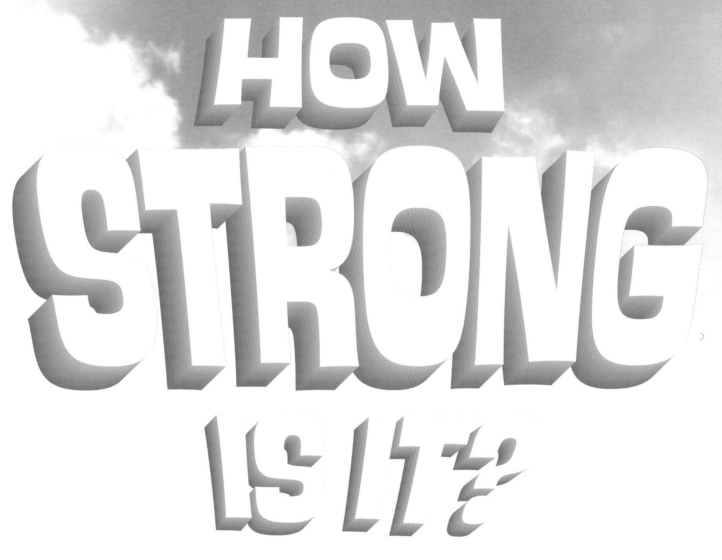

HOW STRONG IS IT?

A Mighty Book All About Strength

by Ben Hillman

SCHOLASTIC REFERENCE
An Imprint of
Scholastic
www.scholastic.com

REVIEW COPY
COMPLIMENTS OF
SCHOLASTIC

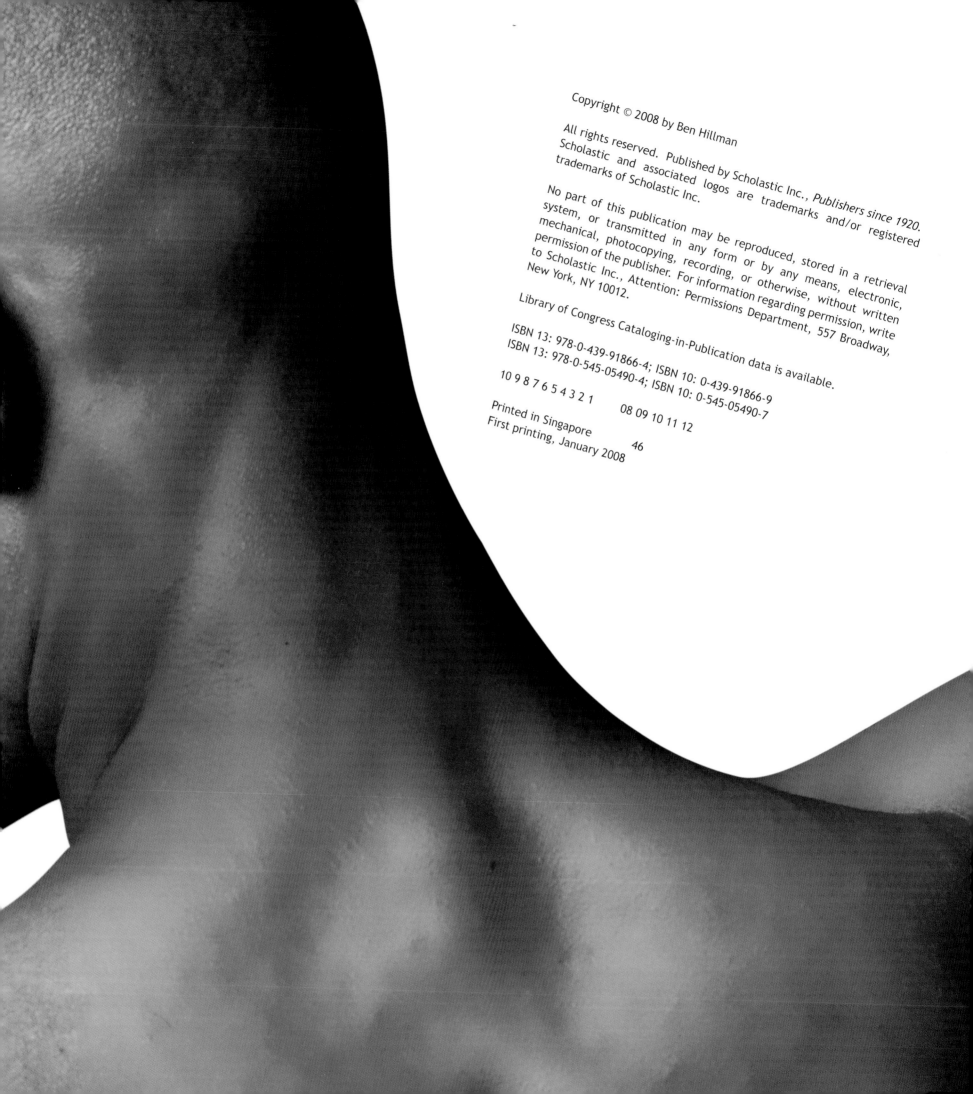

Copyright © 2008 by Ben Hillman

All rights reserved. Published by Scholastic Inc., Publishers since 1920.
Scholastic and associated logos are trademarks and/or registered
trademarks of Scholastic Inc.

No part of this publication may be reproduced, stored in a retrieval
system, or transmitted in any form or by any means, electronic,
mechanical, photocopying, recording, or otherwise, without written
permission of the publisher. For information regarding permission, write
to Scholastic Inc., Attention: Permissions Department, 557 Broadway,
New York, NY 10012.

Library of Congress Cataloging-in-Publication data is available.

ISBN 13: 978-0-439-91866-4; ISBN 10: 0-439-91866-9
ISBN 13: 978-0-545-05490-4; ISBN 10: 0-545-05490-7

10 9 8 7 6 5 4 3 2 1   08 09 10 11 12

Printed in Singapore
First printing, January 2008   46

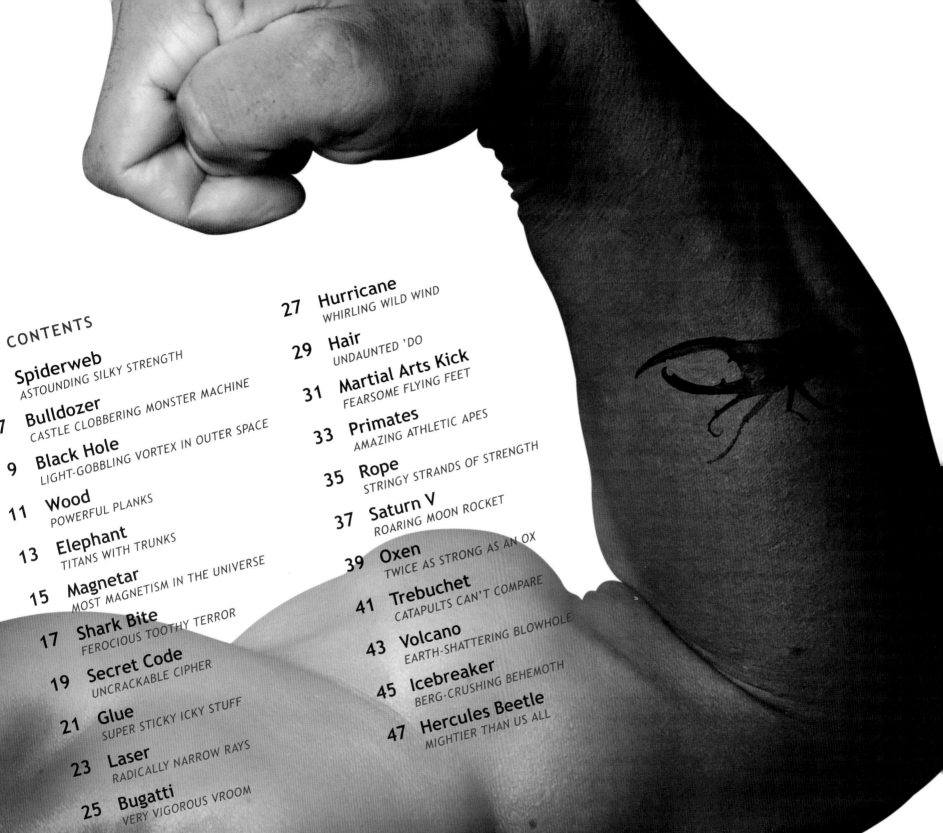

CONTENTS

555 miles per hour
(893 km/h)

600,000 pounds
(272,400 kg)

Spiderweb

Your flight has been delayed.

If a spider could make a web where each silk strand was as thick as a pencil, its web could stop a Boeing 747 in midflight. There is no other substance that even comes close to this stopping power.

Spider silk is the strongest stringlike protein to emerge from the butt of any insect on Earth! But it's much more than that. It's also one of the most amazing materials found on the planet — natural *or* human-made.

Ounce for ounce, spider silk is stronger than nylon and stronger than steel. Not even Kevlar, the world's strongest synthetic fiber — used in bulletproof vests — can match the strength of a web meant to catch flies.

For hundreds of years, scientists have been trying to reproduce the spider's magic in the laboratory but so far without success. Synthetic fibers (like Kevlar) are made using toxic chemicals, heating them to hundreds of degrees and subjecting them to enormous pressures.

The spider does all its labwork in its tiny abdomen without using heat or pressure — and it makes a fiber that's five times stronger than anything humans have produced — all in a blink of an eye. (Or up to eight eyes, if you're counting.)

Now scientists may be close to repro-ducing the spider's genes at the molecular level to make artificial spider silk. So we may actually catch up to what the spider has been doing for a hundred million years.

Meanwhile, just hope the airplane you're riding in doesn't look like a fly.

480,000 pounds
(218,000 kg)

Bulldozer

Castles are some of the biggest, heaviest, strongest buildings ever made. But a castle is no match for the might of the biggest, heaviest, strongest bulldozer in the world — the Komatsu D575A!

The outer walls of a castle may be anywhere from 8 to 20 *feet* thick (2.5 to 6 m) — of solid stone! And yet, this mighty yellow monster can reduce the strongest castle to rubble in a matter of a few days!

For thousands of years, people have been trying to find better, easier ways to move heavy things from place to place. At first, oxen and mules did a lot of this sort of heavy work — and not without some loud complaining.

Then someone figured out how to put a "bull dozer," which was a wide, stout blade, in front of two mules and push earth out of the way. Later, the mules were traded for tractors and the endless loop of metal "caterpillar" tracks were added. Eventually, bright yellow bulldozers were found all over the world.

How strong are these machines? Well, shoveling by hand, you might be able to move a few hundred pounds (kg) per minute — and not very far. But with the strongest bulldozer in the world, the Komatsu D575A, the blade alone can hold up to 90 cubic yards (68 m³) of dirt. Ten scoopfuls of dirt would fill an average house. That's a lot of dirt!

The Komatsu D575A has enough muscle to push more than 480,000 pounds (218,000 kg) of dirt, rocks, or anything else that gets in its way. So the next time you're laying siege to a castle, who you gonna call?

186,282+ miles per second
(299,792+ km/sec)

Black Hole

Gravity sucks.

If you could stand in a black hole with a flashlight (you can't, so don't worry about it), the light wouldn't go anywhere. Why? Because *nothing* escapes the power of gravity in a black hole. Not you. Not Harry Houdini. Not even *light* can escape.

Here's how a black hole happens:

When a star the size of the sun cools off, it collapses suddenly, heats up again, and explodes into a red giant. (Wait another 5 billion years and you'll see.) But what happens when a star many times more massive than the sun cools off and collapses? Its gravity can be so great that when this star collapses, *it keeps right on going*. The giant star gets compressed into an infinitely small point — essentially *right out of the universe* — leaving behind only a humongously powerful gravitational field.

That's a black hole.

But what makes it black? *Escape velocity.* That's the speed an object needs to be travelling to escape a gravitational field.

To escape from Earth's gravity and go into outer space, you must reach a speed of about 7 miles per second (11 km/sec). That's Earth's escape velocity.

To escape from a black hole's gravity you'd have to go *faster than the speed of light* — or 186,282 miles per second (299,792 km/sec). And since *nothing* can go faster than light, escape is impossible.

So if you're a person, a rocket, or a beam of light, this is The End!

(Fade to black.)

160,000 pounds
(73,000 kg)

Wood

Perhaps you have heard of this remarkable material called *wood*. You may have even seen tall plants made of wood called *trees* in your own neighborhood.

You have? Well, you're very lucky because wood is incredible! We are fortunate that there is so much wood in the world, since this is one of the most versatile materials known. And one of the strongest.

Most woods have greater tensile strength and stiffness than steel — that means they're more resistant to stretching and bending.

A single 4-inch (10.2-cm) square post made of black locust wood can support more than 160,000 lbs. (73,000 kg). That's as much as a modest-sized house! (You may not want to balance your house on a single post since it might be a bit wobbly, but you could.)

By the way, black locust is the wood that young Abe Lincoln famously split into fence posts. It's dense, tough and resistant to rot. Different woods have different properties that make them useful in all kinds of applications.

Ash is resistant to shock and is the preferred wood for baseball bats. Old English longbows were made of yew — because it's a natural laminate resistant to repeated bending. Some old windmills were made entirely of wood — even down to the applewood teeth on their gears!

All that strength and versatility comes from one extraordinary kind of plant. And the best part is, this wonderful material grows all by itself, naturally, pollution-free, forever. Can't beat that with a stick.

2,000 pounds
(900 kg)

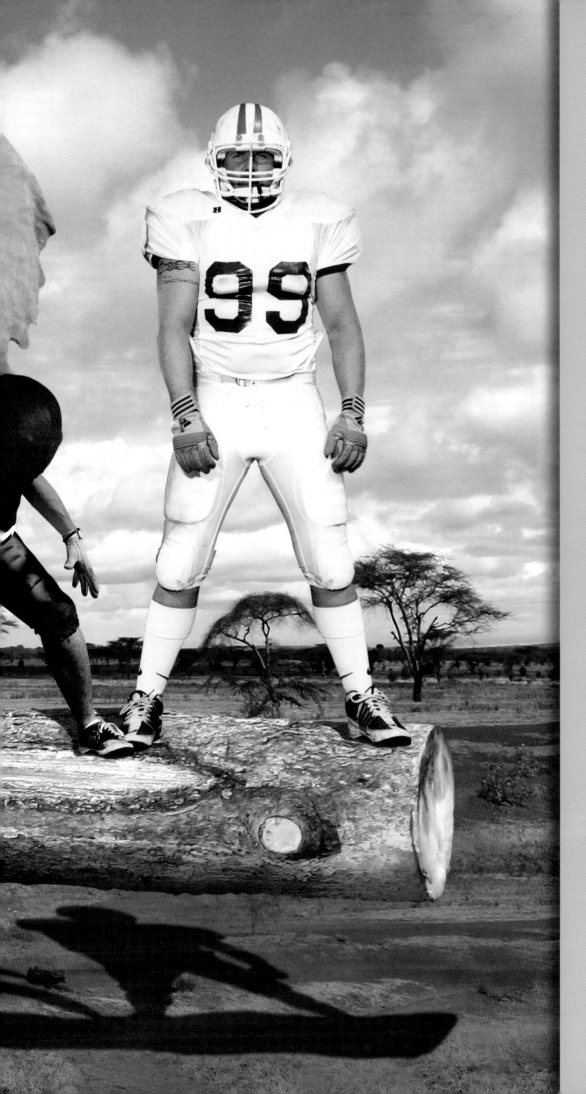

Elephant

Boom! Boom! Boom! Even if you couldn't hear the mighty elephant crashing through the jungle, you could feel it through your feet! Weighing as much as 15,000 pounds (6,800 kg), the elephant is one of the strongest animals alive.

It can drag a load of more than 20,000 pounds (9,000 kg). Using both its tusks and trunk, an elephant can lift more than 2,000 pounds (900 kg)! That's more weight than a hefty log holding four big football players!

For centuries, elephants have been the bulldozers of Southeast Asia. In the forests of Thailand and Myanmar and many other countries in the region, elephants have been trained to carry heavy burdens, to clear land, to move felled trees from the steaming jungle. With mighty legs instead of wheels, elephants don't get stuck in the mud — but they *can* pull stuck trucks out of the mud!

Elephants can run as fast as 30 miles per hour (48 km) when startled or scared, and if that happens, look out! When a herd of elephants starts moving, they pretty much knock down anything in the way!

The great strength of elephants allows them to tear down entire trees just to get at the leaves that would otherwise be too high to reach! In Malaysia, an elephant rampage once destroyed more than 1,000 trees!

But the mighty and magnificent elephant is in danger. Poachers are killing them in huge numbers for their ivory. As a result, the number of elephants in the world is a tiny fraction of what it was, even a few decades ago. Can we save them in time? It's up to us.

1,000,000,000,000,000 gauss

Magnetar

Do you ever feel strangely attracted to a passing neutron star? You most certainly would if that neutron star was a *magnetar* — a star with the most powerful magnetic field in the known universe.

If a magnetar happened to roam to within 50,000 miles (23,000 km) of Earth, and you happened to be wearing braces (yes, some braces are magnetic), the magnetic field would be strong enough to pull you *right off the face of the planet*.

(Actually, there would be other disastrous results if a magnetar came that close to Earth, but we'll ignore them because this girl looks like she's having *such* a good time!)

Magnetic fields are measured in units called *gauss* (rhymes with *mouse*). For instance, the earth's magnetic field is around 0.5 gauss. Not very strong. Just strong enough to make a compass needle flip around.

The sun's magnetic field is around 1 to 5 gauss, but a refrigerator magnet is about 100 gauss!

The most powerful human-made magnetic fields are made with explosives! By setting off explosives around a pulsed magnet, scientists have created a field strength of 10 million gauss — but only for a few microseconds.

Now let's look at the magnetar.

Made of a superfluid of neutrons, weighing as much as eight suns, and compressed to a diameter of 10 miles (16 km), this star can generate a field of 1,000,000,000,000,000 (one *quadrillion*) gauss.

Time to buy a really big refrigerator.

2,300 pounds
(1,043 kg)

Shark Bite

Chainsaws are for wimps.

If you really want to impress your friends with woodchopping power, reach for the nearest shark!

How strong is the bite of the shark? It's oh-so-easy to measure. Just grab your shark, open its mouth, and insert a high accuracy *bite force transducer* (a favorite device of you shark-bite enthusiasts). How does 2,300 pounds (1,043 kg) grab you? With its giant mouth chomping down with this kind of force, a great white shark is capable of snapping through a 6-inch (15-cm) thick chunk of firewood in one bite!

But a shark doesn't even really have to bite that hard to do what has to be done — like tearing chunks off its unfortunate prey or delicately dislodging giant mouth-shaped morsels of surfboard.

That's because of the deadly cutting power of shark teeth. You have one row of teeth, but the great white shark typically has six to eight rows — one row for biting and the other rows ready to come into action whenever a tooth is lost. The largest of those teeth can be more than 3 inches (7.6 cm) long and each tooth is serrated like a steak knife!

How does a human bite compare to a shark's? For humans and sharks of the same size, the bites are about equal! But does that mean you could bite a log in half? Not unless you're the size of a great white. The full chopping power of the shark's bite comes from its size and the sharpness of its teeth. So don't even think about becoming a human chainsaw. Stick to sharks.

65 trillion years

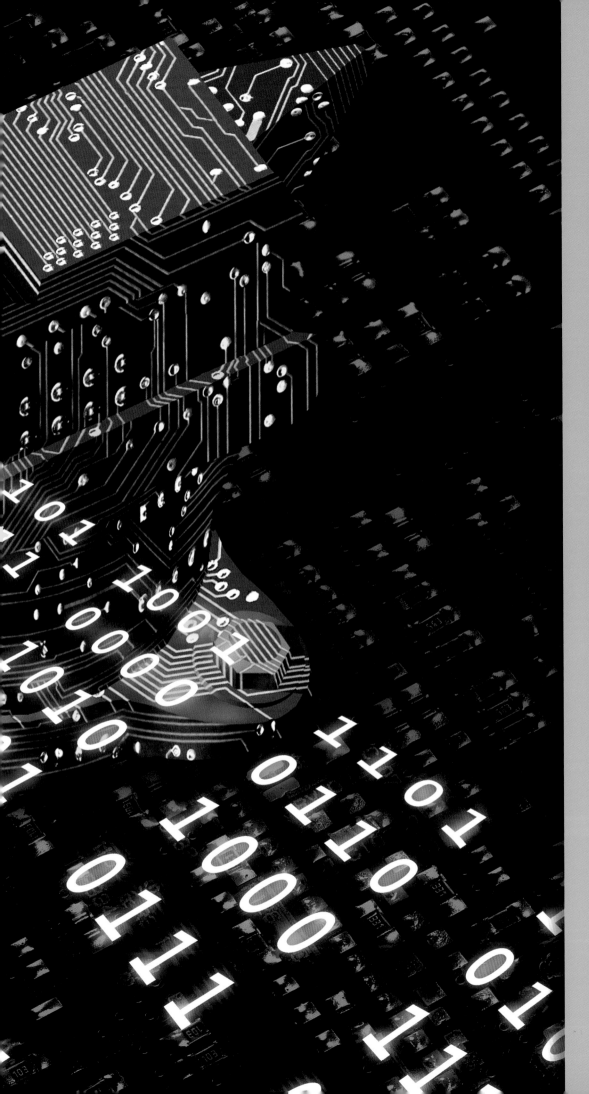

Unbreakable Code

"My name is Bondius. Jamesius Bondius." If you were a secret agent in ancient Rome, you'd probably send your secret message using a code called the *Caesar cipher*. Julius Caesar used a code where every letter of the alphabet was shifted three positions further along in the alphabet. (So A=D, B=E, etc.)

This kind of "displacement" code has 25 possible solutions (using our alphabet) so it's not very hard to crack. But it was good enough for Mr. Caesar in 50 B.C.

In World War II, the Germans used the *Enigma* machine, which used electronics and mechanical rotors to make coded messages. There were 17,576 possible positions for the rotors. But some brilliant people on the Allied side devised high-speed machines to run through all the combinations and break the Enigma code.

Now, in the age of computers, writing secret messages is a whole new ball game. To create "strong crypto," codemakers try to find mathematical methods where there are so many possible keys that even the fastest computers can't plow through them all.

We're not talking about thousands of keys anymore. The last "secure" code was cracked when it was attacked by a computer testing more than 92 billion keys *per second*!

Now there's a new contender for World's Strongest Crypto. It's called AES and the number of possible keys is 2^{128}. How many is that? Well, if computers could run a million times faster than they do now, it would take 65 trillion years to crack AES.

Your secrets are safe. For now.

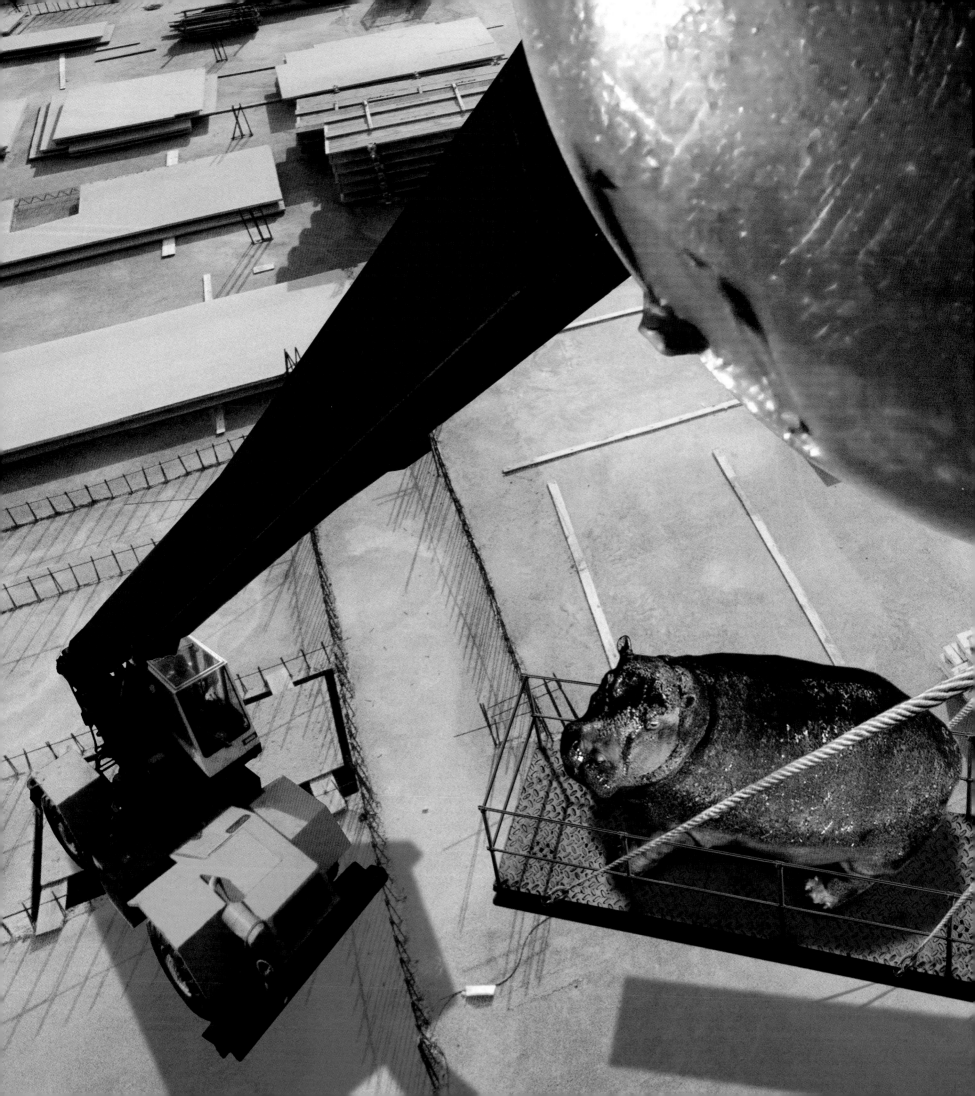

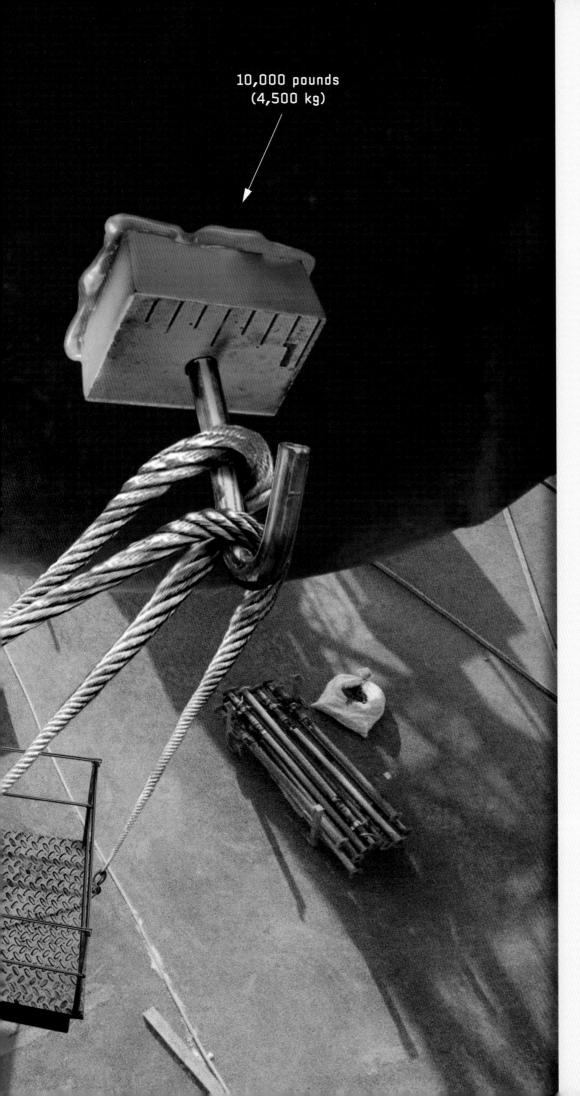

10,000 pounds
(4,500 kg)

Glue

It's the ickiest. It's the stickiest. It's more powerful than any glue ever known. And it's made by tiny bacteria!

These microscopic creatures known as *Caulobacter crescentus* are found in fast-moving rivers, streams, and water pipes. To keep from being washed away by the raging torrent, a *Caulobacter crescentus* clings to river rocks or the insides of pipes with a microscopic stalk. At the end of the stalk are chains of sugar molecules and at the end of those chains are some kind of still-unknown protein molecules that form glue — a glue three times more super than the most super human-made superglue!

If you spread 1 square inch (6.5 cm²) of this glue on the tip of a crane, it could lift a 10,000 pound (4,500 kg) hippopotamus! Try that with your household sticky stuff!

Naturally scientists and engineers are oohing and ahhing over this amazing glue. They're working hard to figure out what exactly these protein glue molecules are, so they can reproduce it in their laboratories.

A glue this strong has countless uses, especially since it sticks even when wet and it's nontoxic. It can be used to make underwater ship repairs and even used as a surgical adhesive.

But there are a few difficulties.

One not-so-minor problem is that this glue adheres to *everything* — including all the tools that would be used to *make* the glue. And, of course, this gloppy water-resistant mess doesn't wash off, either.

Truly a sticky situation.

.8 mile
(1.3 km)

Laser

When you curl up with a good book at night, you usually have a reading lamp a few feet away. That's because if the lamp was any farther, the light would be too dim to read by.

But not if NASA aimed its Geoscience Laser Altimeter System (GLAS) at your book! This laser has such a powerful narrow beam, that if they shone it from .8 miles (1.3 km), the beam would only spread six inches (15 cm). (By the way, don't *ever* shine a laser at or near anyone. Even a small laser pointer.)

You may wonder why your book doesn't catch on fire when the laser is pointed at it. There are many types of lasers for many different purposes. This particular laser is used for bouncing light off things, not cutting, burning or vaporizing. Besides, we don't want to ruin a perfectly good book.

NASA's GLAS laser is part of the Earth Science Enterprise and is used to measure the surface of the Earth and its atmosphere. It can put a 230-foot (70-m) spotlight on Earth from 373 miles (600 km) in space!

The most *powerful* lasers are designed to create thermonuclear fusion — the same process that makes stars burn. At the National Ignition Facility in California, 192 lasers will simultaneously fire their beams on a target less than half an inch across (1 cm), delivering bursts of 500 trillion watts of power in a nanosecond. That's 1,000 times the electric power produced in the entire United States in the same (very short) period of time!

Fusion is a long-sought-after energy source that someday we hope to harness. That will be something to read about!

1,001 horsepower

Bugatti Veyron

It was 1769 and the world was changing. Scottish engineer and inventor James Watt had a hard time convincing people to give up their horses and use his futuristic new steam engine. So to get people to understand the power of his engine, Watt compared it to the force of a horse.

He came up with the word *horsepower* to describe the energy put out by his engine. *This* people understood.

Then came the automobile. This quite innovative device was invented by Karl Benz in Germany in 1886. Powered by gasoline, (which was then available only as a cleaning fluid in pharmacies!), Benz's first car had an engine with a whopping .67 horsepower that could propel the little car along at a blistering speed of 10 miles (16 km) per hour.

Fast-forward to 2005 and the latest improvement in Karl Benz's invention. The Bugatti Veyron 16.4 is, to date, the most powerful production car ever made. Its 8.0-liter, 64-valve, quad-turbo W-16 engine is advertised at "1,001 horsepower" but is really even more than that.

All this power takes the Bugatti Veyron from ignition to 60 miles (97 km) per hour in *2.5 seconds*. At top speed, more than 250 miles (400 km) per hour, you will pass every car on the road in a blur — although you most likely will be breaking the local speed limit.

But all this power does come at a price. At 250 miles (400 km) per hour, you'll use up all your gas in 12 minutes, and the Veyron costs a whopping $1.2 million before taxes.

Come on, pony up!

EARTH

KATRINA
175 mph
(280 km/h)

GREAT RED SPOT
400 mph
(650 km/h)

JUPITER

Hurricane

In August 2005, a storm was brewing. Over the Bahamas, Katrina formed into a mild Category 1 hurricane with winds from 74 to 95 miles (119 to 153 km) per hour. Crossing southern Florida into the Gulf of Mexico, it quickly mushroomed into a ferocious Category 5 hurricane, reaching 500 miles across (800 km), with sustained winds of 175 miles (280 km) per hour.

It was headed straight for New Orleans. This is exactly what people had been fearing for years — a major hurricane making a direct hit on this highly populated area.

By the time Katrina hit the Gulf Coast, it had been downgraded to a Category 3, but the damage it caused was devasting. It battered some 90,000 square miles (233,000 km^2) along the central Gulf Coast of the United States. Merciless winds tore up cities and towns, floods destroyed hundreds of thousands of homes, and 1,836 people lost their lives. It was the costliest natural disaster in the history of the United States.

Amazingly, on Jupiter, Katrina would be a pipsqueak. The massive blotch you see in this photo is called the Great Red Spot. It's a storm that has been raging nonstop for at least 300 years. And it's more than three times wider than the entire planet Earth.

Winds blow counterclockwise around the Great Red Spot at about 400 miles (650 km) per hour — more than the speed of an F6 tornado! Not to mention that Jupiter's tornado-speed hurricane is 16,000 miles (26,000 km) wide!

We're safer on Earth.

17,500 pounds
(8,000 kg)

Hair

Rapunzel! Rapunzel!
Let down your strong hair!

Hang in there, Princes. Rapunzel will see you shortly. Choosy Rapunzel has decided that just one prince won't do. Why have only one eligible bachelor clambering up your golden locks when you can have dozens?

Human hair is strong, but is it really *that* strong? Forsooth, it is. The average human hair can support 2 to 3.5 ounces (60 to 100 g) without breaking. That doesn't sound like much, but the average human head has more than 100,000 hairs. And blondes have more than most. About 140,000 hairs per blonde. (No wonder they get more princes!)

So how many princes can Rapunzel handle? Do the math. Her two golden braids can hold at the very least 17,500 pounds of princes! (That's 8,000 kg if you like your princes metric.)

What makes hair so unbelievably strong? The answer is in its molecules. The main ingredient is a protein called *keratin*, which forms into long chains of amino acids. The long keratin chains are bound together — like rungs in a ladder — by other amino acids containing sulfur. (That's why hair smells so bad when it's burned). These interlocked keratin filaments give hair its incredible strength.

But don't try this at home! We're forgetting one minor detail: How strong is Rapunzel's *scalp*? Although hair really can be this strong, the average scalp is not. Rapunzel must have used the world's strongest glue (see page 21) as shampoo.

Kick

As George Washington used to say in the First Continental Congress: "*Kee-yah!*"

A martial arts kick is one the most fearsome forces that the human body can produce. A well-delivered tae kwon do kick could certainly have cracked the 2,000-pound (908-kg) Liberty Bell.

Force equals mass times acceleration. So the bigger you are, the stronger the force you can deliver. But, if you happen to be not so big, you can use speed to deliver the same impact as someone much bigger. In fact, speed is *twice* as important as mass when delivering a blow. Some martial artists move so fast that they actually have to slow themselves down when they appear in movies so the audience can see what they're doing!

Kicks are stronger than punches, since more of the body is involved in kicking. Surprisingly, tests show that Western-style boxing delivers the most powerful punch — up to 1,000 pounds (454 kg) of force.

But which kind of kick is the most powerful? A kung fu flying double kick can deliver about 1,000 pounds (450 kg) of force. But the most powerful kicks start from the ground. A tae kwon do spinning back kick can deliver more than 1,500 pounds (680 kg) of force. A Muay Thai kick using both arms to hold the opponent's head while delivering a knee strike to the chest, can have the impact of a 35-mile (56-km) per hour car crash!

If only Washington had been a student of Muay Thai, Cornwallis would probably have surrendered a lot sooner.

1,500 pounds (680 kg) of force

1,500 pounds
(680 kg)

Primates

Don't tickle that orangutan!

When you think about how strong people are, you probably think of how much weight we can lift. Well, if you *could* get apes to lift each other (they won't do it, even if you ask nicely), you'd see that the other big primates are a whole lot stronger than we are.

A chimpanzee is very, very close to a person in terms of DNA structure — only about 1 percent different. But that tiny amount makes for big, big differences! A male chimp may only be 4 feet (1.2 m) tall and weigh 132 pounds (60 kg), but it can be four to seven times stronger than a human being. People who think chimps are cute and that they can keep them as pets are often in for a lot of trouble. Most pets can't crush truck tires with their bare hands!

Gorilla muscles may not be well-suited to lifting barbells like ours are, but we could never tear the arms off a gorilla. They can do that to us.

But the real surprise is under the mass of red hair that covers the orangutans. An average orang is stronger than a gorilla! It can even pull open a crocodile's jaw and rip apart the reptile's throat.

Monkeys and great apes spend a lot of time swinging from branches. And it shows. They have absolutely tremendous strength in their hands and fingers. Think of how hard it would be to swing hand over hand from one tree to the next! Yet chimps and orangs can vault from tree to tree with seeming ease all day long! Their grip is naturally strong — it has to be!

14,000 pounds
(6,400 kg)

Rope

What a shame they had to work so hard!

If only the ancient people who built Stonehenge had a few spools of p-phenylene-2 6-benzobisoxazole rigid isotropic crystal polymer fiber ropes, they would have had a much easier time of it.

How did they lift those 14,000-pound (6,400-kg) stones 14 feet (4.3 m) in the air thousands of years ago? No one knows. Nowadays we would use our high-tech rope — a mere 3/8-inch- (1-cm-) thick rope can lift 18,400 pounds (8,354 kg). Diameter-for-diameter, that's stronger than steel!

In fact, a two-inch thick rope made of this same fiber could lift a million pounds (454,000 kg). That's roughly the weight of *all* the stones you see in this photograph!

The use of rope is longer than recorded history — dating to about 19,000 years ago. Then, people used vines, which are a sort of natural rope (think Tarzan). Later, people figured out that by twisting strands of vines and other fibers together they could make it much stronger.

The longest natural rope suspension bridge in the world was built by the Incas in Peru. It was 220 feet (67 m) long and made only from woven grass!

For thousands of years, rope was only made of natural fibers, until the 1950s when synthetic fibers were invented. Now high-tech rope is used to scale the world's highest mountains, sail the world's fastest sailboats, control parachutes and hot-air balloons, and work safely on the sides of skyscrapers.

It's always good to know the ropes.

7,750,000 pounds
(3,500,000 kg)
thrust

Saturn V

The V stands for five.

There were five giant liquid-fueled F-1 rocket engines clustered at the base of the Saturn V moon rocket — the most powerful rocket engines ever made.

Together, the five F-1 engines burned up 11 tons (10 metric tons) of LOX and 5.5 tons (5 metric tons) of kerosene every *second*. That's like emptying an Olympic-size swimming pool full of rocket fuel in less than three minutes. (In case you're wondering, LOX is short for Liquid OXygen. A fuel made of smoked salmon would never have gotten us to the moon.)

The LOX and kerosene fuels mix, ignite, and explode out of the five 12-foot- (3.7-m-) diameter nozzles with a force of 7.75 million pounds (3.5 million kg) of thrust, enough to squoosh the astronauts into their seats like pancakes and hurtle them to outer space.

OK. So we know how powerful the mighty Saturn V rocket is going straight up. But how would it do on the ground?

Here on the Bonneville Salt Flats in Utah, we have strapped a Saturn V rocket to Big Ben, the famous London clock tower and attached some racing tires. The combined weight of the rocket and the clock is around 25 million pounds (11 million kg). How will it perform in a test drive compared to a 6,400-pound (2,900-kg) Hummer H2?

Start your engines.

The Saturn V-powered Big Ben reaches 60 miles per hour (97 km/h) in 8.98 seconds! The Hummer loses — 10.7 seconds.

Now *that's* power.

20,000 pounds
(9,000 kg)

Ox

How strong *is* an ox, anyway?

Forty to fifty average humans could be in a tug-of-war contest against a pair of oxen and *lose*. That's how strong they are. Now you know why oxen have been popular draft animals — used to pull heavy equipment like plows — for thousands of years.

What kind of animal is an ox? Oxen are cows that have been raised and trained as work animals. Typically they are males (since they're bigger) and at least four years old. Oxen must be trained from a young age to do their job and understand the commands of the teamster.

One of the strongest breeds of oxen is the Chianina (pronounced kee-a-nee-na) from central Italy. These mighty white beasts are one of the oldest breeds of oxen in existence. They've been around at least since ancient Roman times. And they're huge! — growing to a size where their shoulder height is more than 6 feet (1.8 m) — and weighing 2,800 pounds (1,300 kg).

Chianina are champion pullers. They usually work in pairs and that's how they're tested in pulling contests. Chianina often win, together pulling more than 20,000 pounds (9,000 kg)! That's the weight of some of the giant 13-foot (4 m) stone statues on Easter Island.

If you've got one of those statues in your backyard, you can just imagine how hard it would be to budge.

To do that, you'd have to be strong — strong as an ox.

130 feet
(40 m)

Trebuchet

How do you get rid of a lousy piano player? Why, with a trebuchet, of course.

How strong is a trebuchet? Well, first, what exactly *is* a trebuchet?

Looking at this ancient throwing machine, it would be easy to confuse the trebuchet with a catapult. But although both were used in war to chuck things great distances, they work differently and the trebuchet is *much* stronger.

While a catapult uses twisted rope to spring the throwing arm forward, the trebuchet relies on gravity and the mass of a huge counterweight to sling objects as heavy as 2,000 pounds (900 kg), either at walls or over walls!

A trebuchet is strong enough to throw a grand piano and its unfortunate companion right onto the roof of Carnegie Hall!

The trebuchet was typically used to attack castles. People inside the castle would simply try to wait until the people outside would get tired and go away. The people outside would either try to knock down the walls, to enter and create total mayhem, or else they would throw disagreeable objects over the walls — such as dead cows and manure, in an attempt to discourage the defenders, or even make them sick.

Most early trebuchets could throw objects only 200 to 300 hundred feet (60 to 90 m). But by the Middle Ages, the range had increased to over a thousand feet (300 m)!

What happened to trebuchets? They were eventually replaced by something even stronger: the gunpowder-fired cannon.

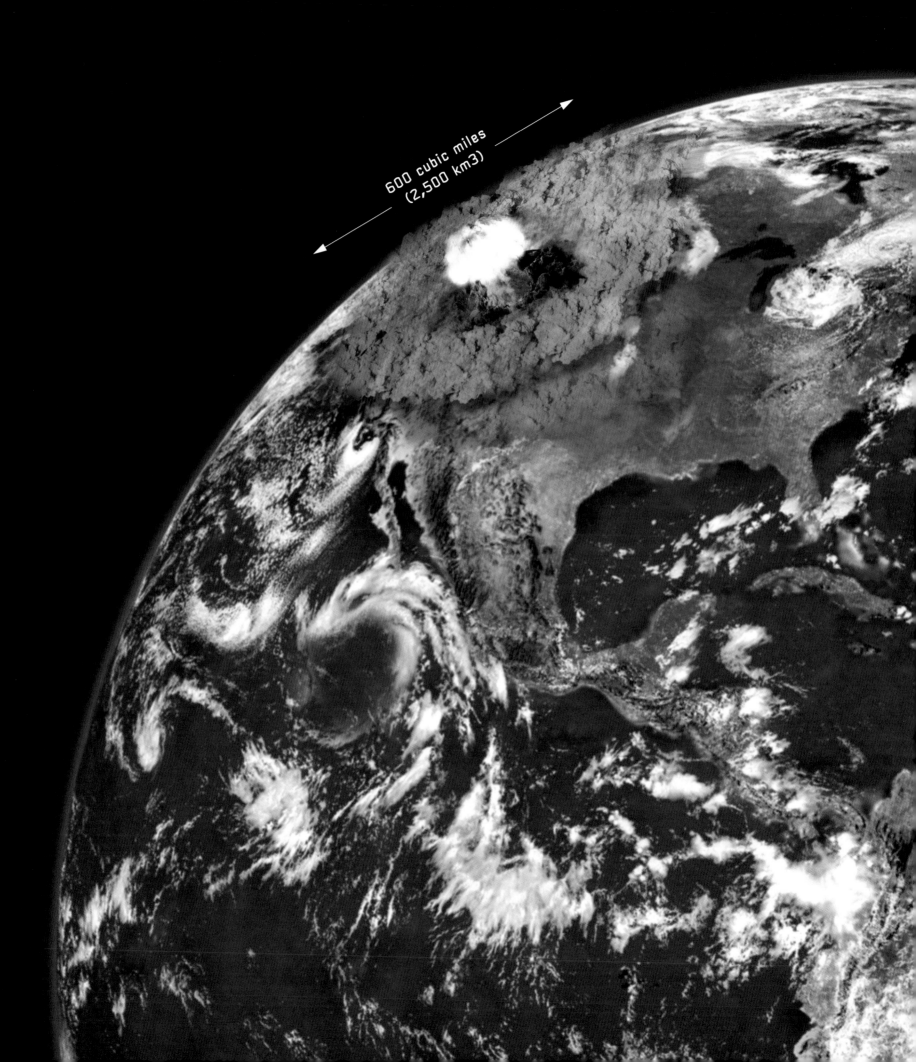

600 cubic miles
(2,500 km3)

Volcano

Visit the natural wonders of beautiful Yellowstone National Park! There's plenty to see and do. Camp, hike, see the spectacular geysers and waterfalls, and take in a grand display of America's wildlife — where grizzlies, wolves, elk, and bison roam free. It's fun for the whole family!

Just remember that 2.1 million, 1.3 million, and 640,000 years ago, the entire park blew up with the force of thousands of atomic bombs in what were possibly the most powerful volcanic explosions in history.

That's right. A few miles beneath the feet of the millions of happy visitors is a colossal pool that is 37 miles (60 km) across and filled with 3,600 cubic miles (15,000 km³) of superhot magma!

Yellowstone is what is called a *caldera volcano*. Instead of a mountain with a hole at the top like a typical volcano, the Yellowstone volcano is a giant underground basin of molten rock with a crust on top. Even today, we can see the ground at Yellowstone rising ever so slightly from year to year as the pressure increases.

2.1 million years ago, the crust could no longer contain the enormous pressure and *boom*! Yellowstone exploded with 600 cubic miles (2,500 km³) of debris vaulting into the atmosphere. That's enough volcanic ejecta to cover the entire western United States in *4 feet* (1.2 m) of ash and rock — 6,000 times greater than the volume released in the 1980 eruption of Mount Saint Helens, Washington.

Now Yellowstone is resting peacefully. So enjoy your visit. But tread lightly.

СОВЕТСКИЙ СОЮЗ

75,000
horsepower

Icebreaker

This is the icebreaker they call when *other* icebreakers get stuck in the ice. The *Sovetsky Soyuz*, along with its fire-engine red Russian sister ships, are the most powerful icebreakers in the world. Their job is to lead convoys of cargo vessels across the top of the world by smashing shipping lanes through the frozen Arctic.

Two nuclear reactors, each delivering 171 megawatts of power, drive the huge screws which propel the ship with a force of 75,000 horsepower through massive ice floes *15 feet* (4.6 m) thick. But breaking ice isn't just about brute force. Modern icebreakers are designed to actually ride up on top of the ice floes and then break them with their massive weight. Underwater, air bubbles are pumped out around the hull to reduce friction.

When smashing through thick ice, the *Sovetsky Soyuz* uses up 11 ounces (312 g) per day of highly enriched uranium. She carries 1,100 pounds (550 kg) of the stuff — enough to sail for five years without refueling.

In 1991, the *Sovetsky Soyuz* was the first ship to ever take tourists to the North Pole. Sailing across the top of the world from Murmansk, Russia, to Nome, Alaska, she was also the first to complete a transpolar voyage.

Aside from ferrying tourists around, the *Sovetsky Soyuz* also serves science. Nowadays, as the polar sea ice is melting due to climate change, the vessel takes scientists deep into the polar icepack, so they can try to understand how the current warming trends might affect the whole planet.

37 pounds
(17 kg)

Hercules Beetle

The Champion of Champions! The One and Only! The Strongest Animal in the World!

Not the gorilla, not the elephant, not even the great blue whale can match the mightiest member of the animal kingdom.

It's *Dynastes hercules* — the greatest of the rhinoceros beetles!

Pound for pound, ounce for ounce, gram for gram, this awesome creature from the rain forests of Central and South America can outlift any being on Earth. Hercules may be small for a world champion weight lifter, but compared to the other 400,000 kinds of beetles, it's one of the largest. Male Hercules beetles sometimes reach a length of up to 6.75 inches (17 cm).

That's a still a lot smaller than what you probably imagine for World's Strongest Animal. But Hercules' power dwarfs even an 11,000 pound (5,000 kg) elephant! An Asian elephant can carry up to 25 percent of its own weight on its back. That's nothing. The ant, also famous for its strength, can carry around thirty times its own weight. Pretty impressive, but strictly second-place material.

Now for the gold medalist! Presenting that most ferocious horned mini-monster — the Hercules beetle! Weighing in at just three quarters of an ounce (20 grams), it can carry a jaw-dropping *37 pounds* (17 kg). That comes to an awesome *850 times* its own weight.

So drop your puny barbells, you miserable humanoid weaklings! Bow down! The Mightiest Animal stands here before you!

Index

Credits

3,48 Man: Les Byerley/iStockphoto; Tattoo:
Richard Sands
5 Jet: Dreamstime.com
7 Castle: Marlee/Dreamstime.com; Bulldozer:
courtesy of Binder Machinery Company for Komatsu
America Corp.; Knight: Firehorse/iStockphoto;
Sky: James Warren/iStockphoto
9 Boy: Richard Sands
11 Ben Hillman
13 Elephant: Nightowlza/Dreamstime.com; Football
Players: Wolfgang Lienbacher/iStockphoto, Fredrick
Clement/GettyImages, B.Bird/zefa/Corbis; Log: Ben
Hillman; Background: Christian Domes/iStockphoto
15 Girl: Richard Sands; House: Justin Horrocks/
iStockphoto; Objects: Kate Lampro; Landscape:
Ben Hillman
17 Shark: Stephen Frink/GettyImages; Guys: Richard
Sands; Background: Ben Hillman, Richard Sands
19 Robert U. Taylor, Ben Hillman
21 Hippo: Creatas/Fotosearch; Crane: Lonnie Duka/
Index Stock Imagery; Wrecking Ball: Ellis Martin/
World of Stock; Background: Helen King/Corbis
23 Girl: Richard Sands; Cityscape: Sri Prasad
Tadimalla/iStockphoto
25 Car: courtesy of Bugatti Automobiles SAS,
Dorlisheim, France; Horses: Arturo Limon/
iStockphoto, Holly Kuchera/iStockphoto, Geoff
Kuchera/iStockphoto; Background: Ann Piaia/
Dreamstime.com
27 Jupiter: NASA/JPL; Earth: NASA/Visible Earth
29 Rapunzel, Princes, Tower: Richard Sands;
Background: Ben Hillman
31 Martial Artist: Eastwestimaging/Dreamstime.com;
Bell: Gmv/Dreamstime.com; Background: Hblamb/
Dreamstime.com
33 Orangutan: Lisa F. Young/iStockphoto; Gorilla:
Erick Paez/iStockphoto; Chimpanzee: Mark Owens/
iStockphoto; Human: Photoshow/Dreamstime.com;
Background: Ben Hillman
35 Stonehenge: Emble/Dreamstime.com; Man:
Amy Rudnick
37 Rocket: NASA/Roger Ressmeyer/Corbis; Big Ben:
Mairead/Dreamstime.com; Background: Vespergo/
Dreamstime.com
39 Oxen: courtesy of Drew Conroy Ph.D., Oxwood
Farm, Berwick, Maine; Statue: Michal Wozniak/
iStockphoto; Background: javarman3/iStockphoto
41 Piano, Pianist: Richard Sands; Trebuchet:
Lagui/Dreamstime.com; Violinist: Hélène Vallée/
iStockphoto, Ken Hurst/iStockphoto; Background:
Ben Hillman
43 Earth: NASA/Visible Earth
45 Ship: courtesy of Quark Expeditions; Background:
Cay-Uwe Kulzer/iStockphoto
47 Beetle, Barbell, Podium: Richard Sands; Crowd:
Brian Poirier/iStockphoto; Background: Joshua Blake/
iStockphoto

Special Thanks: James Akers, Luke Ban,
Donna Barfield, Michael Connelly, Emily Crawford,
Jeff Dilks, Kerry Douglas, Ethan Ellenberg,
Tony Gualtieri, Marina Germain, Dr. Alice Harding,
Dr. David Hillman, Dr. Manny Hillman,
Dwayne Howard, Dr. Daniel R. Huber, Tom Ingersoll,
Kate Lampro, Paula Manzanero, Ellen Maggio,
Madeleine Maggio, Peter Maggio, Dan Mahoney,
Emerson Martin, Garnet Ord, Amy Rudnick,
Richard Sands, Darrel Schoeling, Jim Spieler,
Bill Steigerwald, Robert U. Taylor, Becky Terhune,
David Turnbough, Lindsay Turner.